WHAT DO THEY DO? WHAT DO THEY DO? WHAT DO THEY DO?

WHAT DO THEY DO?
FIREFIGHTERS

BY JENNIFER ZEIGER

CHERRY LAKE Publishing

Published in the United States of America by Cherry Lake Publishing
Ann Arbor, Michigan
www.cherrylakepublishing.com

Content Adviser: Daniel Young, Fire Chief, Waukegan Fire Department
Reading Adviser: Cecilia Minden-Cupp, PhD, Literacy Consultant

Photo Credits: Cover and pages 1, 9, and 15, ©Monkey Business Images, used under license from Shutterstock, Inc.; page 5, ©iStockphoto.com/matsou; page 7, ©Dariush M., used under license from Shutterstock, Inc.; page 11, ©Four Oaks, used under license from Shutterstock, Inc.; page 13, ©Gemenacom/Dreamstime.com; page 17, ©Kim D. French, used under license from Shutterstock, Inc.; page 19, ©Peterphoto7/Dreamstime.com; page 21, ©Kevin Britland/Alamy

LIBRARY OF CONGRESS CATALOGING-IN-PUBLICATION DATA
Zeiger, Jennifer.
  What do they do? Firefighters / by Jennifer Zeiger.
     p. cm.—(Community connections)
  Includes bibliographical references and index.
  ISBN-13: 978-1-60279-804-5 (lib. bdg.)
  ISBN-10: 1-60279-804-4 (lib. bdg.)
  1. Fire extinction—Vocational guidance—Juvenile literature. 2. Fire fighters—Juvenile literature. I. Title. II. Title: Firefighters.
  TH9119.Z45 2010
  363.37023—dc22   2009042800

Cherry Lake Publishing would like to acknowledge the work of The Partnership for 21st Century Skills. Please visit *www.21stcenturyskills.org* for more information.

Printed in the United States of America
Corporate Graphics Inc.
July 2010
CLFA07

FIREFIGHTERS

CONTENTS

WHAT DO THEY DO?

FIGHTING THE FLAMES

You are at school when the fire alarm goes off. You and your classmates follow your teacher outside. A large red fire truck is there.

The firefighters have come! They will make sure everyone is safe and sound.

Firefighters often arrive in bright red trucks.

Firefighters are **first responders**. This means they arrive first at fires and other **emergencies**. Medical workers and firefighters help one another.

Firefighters must act quickly. They always keep their tools ready.

Firefighters get to emergencies as fast as they can.

THINK!

Why do firefighters have to act so quickly? Fire spreads rapidly. People might be hurt. Getting to a fire quickly can save lives. But firefighters do more than fight fires. How do you think being fast helps in other emergencies?

7

Firefighters depend on teamwork. Everyone has a job to do. Some firefighters are in charge of water hoses or ladders.

Other firefighters look for people who need help. They use **Halligan tools** and axes to break through walls or windows. The **fire chief** and other officers make sure everyone stays safe.

Firefighters listen to instructions.

Fires are **dangerous**. Firefighters use special equipment to stay safe. Coats and pants are called **turnouts**. These protect the firefighters from the fire's heat. Helmets, gloves, and boots protect them from sharp or falling objects.

Firefighters also have masks hooked up to air tanks. These masks help them breathe in rooms filled with smoke.

Firefighting can be dangerous work.

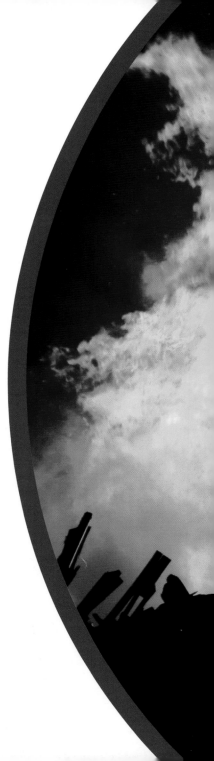

LIFE AT THE STATION

Fire trucks and tools are kept in a fire station. Firefighters clean and check all their tools. They study ways to prevent and fight fires. They work out to stay in shape.

Firefighters keep their equipment ready to go.

Are you ready to go if there is a fire? Make a list of things you should do. What number do you call? How do you get outside safely? Where will you meet outside? Practice what to do with your family.

Firefighters often live at the station while **on duty**. Most stations have kitchens. Firefighters can cook meals.

There are also places for firefighters to rest or sleep. This way, firefighters have their tools close by. They are ready to answer a call.

At the station, firefighters may talk and relax.

KEEPING PEOPLE SAFE

Firefighters do more than fight fires. They help when someone is sick or injured.

Firefighters also help during major **disasters**. There might be a flood or earthquake. Firefighters rescue people. They stay to help clean up.

Firefighters use boats to rescue people in the water.

RESCUE

Most firefighters work for a city or town. Others might work at airports. Some are trained to fight forest fires.

Smaller towns might have **volunteer** firefighters. These people usually have other jobs. They take turns being on call to fight fires.

Some firefighters battle forest fires from the air. They drop materials on the fires to put them out.

19

ASK QUESTIONS!

Do you want to learn more about firefighters? Try talking to some! They can tell you about the job. Maybe you will be a firefighter one day!

Firefighters also teach people about fire safety. They might visit schools or neighborhoods. They talk about ways to prevent fires. They also tell us what to do if there is a fire.

Firefighting is not easy. Firefighters risk their lives every day to keep us safe!

Firefighters talk to people about fires and staying safe.

RELEASE CHARGER LEAD ↓

L COUNTY
FIRE BRIGADE

21

GLOSSARY

dangerous (DAYN-jur-uhss) likely to cause harm

disasters (dih-ZASS-turz) events that cause much damage and loss

emergencies (ee-MUR-juhn-seez) sudden and dangerous situations that need immediate action

fire chief (FYR CHEEF) the person in charge of a fire department

first responders (FURST ree-SPON-durz) people trained to provide immediate help in an emergency

Halligan tools (HAHL-ih-guhn TOOLZ) special tools made for many uses, including opening windows and car doors and breaking through walls

on duty (AHN DOO-tee) at work

turnouts (TURN-outs) a firefighter's specially made coat and pants

volunteer (vol-uhn-TEER) a person who does a job, usually without pay

FIND OUT MORE

BOOKS

Ames, Michelle. *Firefighters in Our Community*. New York: PowerKids Press, 2010.

Leake, Diyan. *Firefighters*. Chicago: Heinemann Library, 2008.

WEB SITES

City of Davis California Fire Department: Firefighter Protective Clothing Tour
http://cityofdavis.org/Fire/pct/
Read more about what a firefighter wears and why.

Fire Prevention Canada: Safety Tips for the Home
www.fiprecan.ca/index.php?section=2&show=homeTips
Learn all about fire safety in your home.

INDEX

ABOUT THE AUTHOR

Jennifer Zeiger graduated from DePaul University. She now lives in the Chicago area with her two cats. She would like to thank Ross Usmani for his help in learning more about firefighters.

24